The
College
Experience

Kaylah Marie

ISBN-13: 978-0692876442 (KBCreations)

ISBN-10: 0692876448

DEDICATION

This book is dedicated to anyone who has ever been told their dream was unrealistic in any shape, form, or fashion.

CONTENTS

ACKNOWLEDGMENTS

Thank you to everyone following their dreams.

Introduction

Many people come to college with the idea that earning a degree will guarantee a successful future. Unfortunately, there are no guarantees to success by attending college. However, the countless opportunities for personal and professional growth during the experience, greatly increase the probability of finding future success.

As I prepared to graduate college, I recalled the events that took place within my four years as an undergraduate student. I thought about how much easier life might have been if I had a better idea of what to expect going in. This book is intended to be used as a guide, to help ease the transition into college for current and prospective college students.

"My mission in life is not merely to survive, but to thrive; and to do so with some passion, some compassion, some humor, and some style."
-Marguerite "Maya" Angelou

Reintroduction

I came to college to earn a degree,
Not only that but I wanted to explore.
I'll stop to acknowledge the poetry here,
Reading this book shouldn't feel like a chore.

My first year in college I had a set plan,
I was sure of what I wanted to do.
After being exposed to new ways of thinking,
I became indecisive and lacked even the slightest clue.

Fast forward to senior year,
I narrowed down my list of aspirations.
Writing a book to explain the college experience,
Exceeded my own expectations.

Self-Introductions

Self-introductions give students an opportunity to distinguish themselves from everyone else. Having a general idea of what self-introductions entail can improve the confidence needed to perform them successfully. The most common self-introductions incorporate a name, background, and a variation of interests and goals.

Stating your name clearly and confidently can go a long way. It can create a sense of self-assurance that sets the tone for the rest of the introduction speech. Equally, practicing your name out loud and in front of a mirror can help build charisma and relieve some of the anxiety that can be attributed to public speaking.

Background information included in a self-introduction pertain to personal facts that most people wouldn't mind having a conversation about later. This usually includes divulging things such as what city you are from, or how many siblings you might have. These statements are brief and give the audience a general idea of who you are and where you come from. In addition, background information can be interesting and create a sense of community when participants are fully engaged, enabling them to recognize the similarities amongst the group.

The common goals and interests discussed during self-introductions throughout the college experience pertain to future career goals. This part of the self-introduction might come easy if you are aware of what you plan to do in the future. However, this task can become somewhat difficult if you are unsure of what the future holds. Because it is not uncommon to be unsure of future career goals in a college environment, simply expressing the uncertainty of your future will be the easiest and most accepted response.

"If you have an opportunity to use your voice you should use it."
-Samuel L. Jackson

Don't Sweat It

Don't worry about self-introductions,
Compared to the rest of college, they're cake.
You should already know all about yourself,
There's not much room for mistake.

Introductions aren't always easy,
That's not what I'm trying to say.
Announcing first name, year, and major,
Isn't usually why people's hair tends to gray.

Networking

Networking is simply the act of connecting with people. Making connections with people in college can mean having a friend in class to study with or having a professional reference for a new job. Having several contacts throughout college can be advantageous in and out of the classroom.

Networking with classmates can be beneficial for several reasons. When you get to know the people in your classes it becomes easier to share notes and create study groups for future exams. Because everyone takes notes differently, there is also a chance to pick up new techniques about studying and note taking that can increase chances of success. Having contact information for classmates can also be beneficial to stay on top of current assignments if you ever have a reason to miss class.

Many professors encourage students to speak with them about course work, but also don't mind being a resource beyond class material. Professors appreciate when students ask questions and are almost always willing to meet one on one to explain material despite large class sizes. It might seem intimidating to approach a professor face to face, with that being said, communicating through email can be just as effective.

When it comes to networking for jobs and internships, for starters it is good to research opportunities available in your intended field. If you're planning on getting an internship working with animals for example, take a trip to the zoo or the humane society to find out who's willing to offer you an opportunity or simply lead you in the right direction.

"When a smile breaks open into laughter hearts open! Laughter created space, ease, and connection. It reveals our true nature. Laughter is our soul's joy song. What could be sexier than a song our souls move to?"
–Tracee Ellis Ross

Connect

Networking is very important,
Essentially, it's all about who you know.
Even if the connection isn't strong,
A familiar face in a job interview can be the difference between a "yes" or a "no".

Introduce yourself to your professors,
It shows them that you care.
Even if it's just one question on an assignment,
By reaching out for help you might find serious advantages there.

Introduce yourself to classmates,
You never know who you might meet.
It's a chance the future President is right next to you,
Sitting in the adjoined lecture seat.

Dress up often and drop into various professional events,
Take advantage of free cookies and punch.
Make a nametag and wear a smile,
You might end up discussing job opportunities over lunch.

Awkward moments

Awkward moments in college can be comical and harmless, or crude and heart breaking. They can turn into your wildest dream or your worst nightmare. Being able to see an awkward moment coming, is the best way to come out on top. If you pay attention, you'll find that the most random, embarrassing, or memorable moments are usually considered "awkward".

Some situations in college can trigger strong emotions and opinions that can create an uncomfortable environment. In these circumstances, it is important is remove personal feelings in the matter and be completely open to what emotions and opinions are being expressed around you. Being aware of what is being expressed around you makes it easier to decide if the situation is worth addressing or not. The situation is only worth addressing if you have a desire to change the atmosphere and also believe your efforts will be worthwhile. If you don't have any desire to make a change or feel that your input won't make a difference, it is better to stay quiet to avoid unnecessary conflict. An uncomfortable moment only becomes awkward if the passion isn't proven.

Some of the most memorable moments that are experienced in college have some inkling of awkwardness to them. Awkward moments can happen behind closed doors, or on national news. You might never see them coming, but once they've happened, they might end up being an experience you may never forget.

"Our future is our confidence and self-esteem." –Tupac Shakur

Heads Up

Awkward moments are life's curve ball,
A popular pitch known as humiliation.
The best strategy is to stay alert,
Swing with perspective and follow through with the power of imagination.

I used to be uncomfortable being the only girl,
Surrounded by boys in classes who looked at me weird.
I chalked it up to my beautifully unpredictable feminine nature,
It creates an atmosphere around me to be feared.

I assumed American slavery was to blame for my discomfort and pain,
Institutional racism, mass incarceration, cruelty, and hate.
White washing of history, lost ties to ancestry, and lack of knowledge,
I blame for past, present, and future masses' mindset to discriminate.

I would never agree that war could ever be an effective strategy,
If the goal is to stop violence and promote peace.
Permanent displacement, poverty, sickness, and death,
War encourages terror and allows widespread devastation to inevitably increase.

Changing Majors

The degree received based on a selected major gives a potential employer an idea of what you know and how it can be applied to the field. The major you choose doesn't always have to be specifically related to the ideal career choice, but it helps for the major to have some relation to the area of interest.

When considering changing majors, it is important to be aware of how that will impact your current academic career track. Depending on the hours already completed for the current major, changing majors may shorten or lengthen the time it takes to complete your degree program. The original major may be related to the intended major, in the sense that it may not have an impact on the time span of your college experience. However, if the major you intend to switch to has no relation to the original major, there may be additional time added to your college career due to the additional class requirements needed to complete the new degree program.

Changing majors can be beneficial if the new major is more specific to the intended career. It can allow for increased knowledge and skills needed to be successful on the new career path. However, if changing majors will not improve specific knowledge on a topic or improve chances of finding a job in the intended field, changing majors may not be beneficial in the long run. Adding a minor or enrolling in interesting classes as electives can be an alternative to starting a new degree program.

There are a wide variety of subjects that colleges offer and the chances of discovering new areas of interest are high. Changing majors is an option that should be considered whenever the current degree program no longer meets your career or academic needs. However, if changing majors will significantly increase the career time or course load, you may want to re-evaluate the purpose for the change. Even if changing majors isn't necessary, taking up new areas of interest on your own time is always advantageous.

"Intelligence plus character—that is the goal of true education."
–Martin Luther King Jr.

4 Year Plan

Business was my first major,
For various reasons that's where it all started.
After losing interest within the first week,
I thought it would be wise if the business major and I parted.

Law school was the end goal,
Hence a Political Science major made sense.
Unfortunately, I didn't find an interest in the core material,
Not to mention I thought discussing politics was pastime for the dense.

Healthcare Law was my specific career goal,
Changing my major to Health Science seemed right.
I was changing majors for a third time,
Who knew the decision would be such a difficult plight.

A Bachelors of Health Science in Health Science,
The official title of my undergraduate degree.
Because I was so adamant on graduating in four years,
Changing majors wasn't an option after three.

Breaks

A break is the time away from a routine or project intended to give a sense of clarity and a peace of mind. When breaks aren't taken during times of stress or continuous activity, it can take a toll on the brain as well as the body. With that being said, breaks during the college experience should be taken regularly. Although there are scheduled breaks within the academic calendar, incorporating unofficial breaks during strenuous activities can decrease the feeling of being overwhelmed, which hinders the ability to perform at full potential. When planning a break you should always consider where, when, and how to ensure you are using the time wisely.

The work environment alone can be the cause of stress. If the activity at hand is something that has been done quietly in an isolated area for an extended period of time, an effective break would include fresh air and company. On the other hand, if an activity is loud and fast paced, finding somewhere calm and quiet would be best.

Breaks don't need to be long to be successful. The more time you have for a break, the better, but short breaks can be just as effective. Setting an alarm for a short time and going to do something to relax until the alarm goes off is a good way to make a short break worthwhile. Worrying about the remaining time of a break can keep you from reaping the full benefits of it.

The time and environment of a break won't matter if you don't use it to rest. When an activity takes a lot of brain power like writing a paper or doing research, the best activity to do would be something that gives your brain a chance to rejuvenate. Going for a walk or taking a nap are both examples of things that can be done for any amount of time without causing too much strain on the brain. When deciding on what to do during a break it always helps if it is enjoyable compared to the previous activity.

"The hardest thing to do is to be true to yourself, especially when everybody is watching." -Dave Chappelle

Work Smart

Sometimes it's necessary to step away,
For the sake of your own sanity.
Constant stress leads to mental exhaustion,
A preventable self-inflicted calamity.

Sleep is appropriate sometimes,
It's not the only way the brain can rest.
Physical activity like going to the gym can recharge the mind,
This can help with focus if you have been studying profusely to pass a test.

Timed intervals between work and rest,
A method good for long periods of study.
The idea is to work for an hour straight,
Take thirty minutes to chat or grab lunch with a buddy.

Productivity should set the standard,
The indication for when a break is due.
If focusing on the task becomes uncomfortable in any way,
This should be taken as an undeniable clue.

Travel Opportunities

Traveling anywhere outside of your regular surroundings creates the potential for an exciting learning experience. Exploring the community, signing up for volunteer events, and planning trips throughout the semesters, can help keep college interesting.

Many colleges and universities are built in the middle of an already established community. Even "college towns", have local communities that will offer opportunities for new experiences. Local parks, trails, restaurants, museums, and art galleries include some of the many new places to visit when moving to college.

Volunteer events can also create opportunities to travel. There are many sponsored volunteer events that give students a chance to visit new regions nationally and internationally. During this time you will be able to experience a wide variety of new people, places, and cultures. Volunteering to help others can always prove to be a rewarding experience for all parties involved.

With proper planning, regular trips to exciting destinations can be one of the best parts of the college experience. Weekend road trips can be a great way to experience nearby amusement parks or popular attractions. The scheduled time off during the semesters can also create the perfect opportunities to travel. It's never too soon to start planning a trip. If you think of a great place to spend the week of spring break before the first day of fall semester, it's a good idea to mark off the days on a calendar and figure out what is needed to turn that dream into a reality.

"You can't understand most of the important things from a distance."
-Bryan Stevenson

Save the Date

I have always dreamed of traveling the world,
It's actually my greatest passion.
Even as I think about it now,
There's a fire in my chest burning furiously like you couldn't imagine.

I knew I wanted to experience new places,
Going away for college was the first step that I took.
I never thought by traveling two hours west of my home town,
I would get the opportunity to visit places I'd scene in movie or had read about in a book.

I went to Tybee Island, Georgia my freshman year,
It was my first time on a beach.
There I was introduced to the meaning of beauty and peace,
Lessons I will argue only the ocean can teach.

New restaurants enhance the quality of travel,
Roscoe's Chicken and Waffles had the best waffle I might ever eat.
Bubba Gump Shrimp serves the most delicious burger,
Made of mushroom, no meat.

The air was cold on the edge of Pike's Peak,
I was surrounded by the Rocky Mountains at almost 14,000 feet.
A view I would encourage everyone to seek,
It's a transformative experience to witness Heaven and Earth meet.

I skated on the Venice Beach Boardwalk,
An experience I always knew would be fate.
It was Spring Break of my junior year,
I got to experience the warmth of California, America's Golden State.

Books

Some classes have required books that may never be used. With that being said, if you are afraid of wasting money on a book in fear that it might collect dust all semester, it's wise to plan ahead. It is best to go over the class syllabus and determine if there are any required readings in the first few weeks of class. This can give you an initial idea of the necessity of the book. If you get through the first exam and haven't used the text book at all, chances are it might not be necessary. Some professors provide printouts of the text to save you the trouble of buying the book, and others tell you on the first day that you'll be completely fine without it.

If you end up purchasing the book, it doesn't make sense not to put it to use. Going over what you learned in class, while also reading the lessons in the text can help get a better understanding of the material. This task also greatly increases the chance of doing well in the class. Buying a book you never use, for a class that you end up failing, can be tough to say the least.

Books are great tools inside and outside of the classroom. Reading books that relate to class is important. However, finding good books to read in your free time can prove to be just as valuable. Reading books about interesting people and places assist with your understanding of yourself and the world around you. There is ample time in college to read. Finding a good book every now and then throughout the semester can reduce stress, expand vocabulary, and improve analytical thinking abilities.

"Words are our most inexhaustible source of magic." –J.K. Rowling

How?

It's funny that people can say,
They don't like, or even hate reading.
It's funny like how I'd laugh if I got a paper cut,
And it wouldn't stop bleeding.

I actually don't know where I'd be,
If I wasn't able to read.
Would I even know of my ancestors,
Who died for such a want, which could be arguably a need?

Reading goes beyond words,
It is an expression of the power of the mind.
To see a story or witness a journey all in your head,
A phenomenon nothing short of Divine.

I have read the story of Santiago by Paulo Coelho,
I was there when he discovered his treasure.
His journey was long and arduous,
But reading about the adventures of an Alchemist gave me great pleasure.

I read the Letter to My Daughter,
Along with other brilliant pieces by Maya Angelou.
Now it makes me wonder if I wasn't able to read,
Would I have such an appreciation for the way in which words flow?

I read to learn about things I don't know,
As well as gain an understanding of things I can't see.
Reading has proved to me above all else,
How spectacular the human experience is meant to be.

Dorms

Living in a dorm can be the most exciting experience in college. Dorms may have a theme or interest area that allow students to get involved and participate in various activities throughout the semester. Being a resident in the dorms can give students an opportunity to meet new people, find out about exciting opportunities around campus, and experience what it's like to live independently.

Students in the same dorm usually share some of the same classes. This is the perfect opportunity to get to know dormmates and start study groups. In addition to study groups, it is also beneficial to know multiple people in the dorms when it comes to planning movie and game nights. The more people you get involved the more fun there is to be had. More importantly, knowing people around the dorm can be a great way to save money on food. If everyone can pitch in to pay for take-out, or cook a dish to add to a meal, it cuts the price and can increase the variety of food options.

While living in the dorms, students will always be able to find out about interesting events happening around campus. Poster boards and weekly newsletters sent to students, are some of the ways dorms help students keep up to date with what's going on around campus. Word of mouth works well as students are constantly looking for new members to join or participate in various events. Dorm living is one of the easiest ways to find out about the many opportunities your college has to offer.

"Education is our passport to the future, for tomorrow belongs to the people who prepare for it today." –Malcolm X

Play Place

Living in the dorms made for a good start,
I got to experience what it's like having my own space.
The major facilities are shared,
Other than that, in a way I had my own place.

Community bathrooms are cleaned daily,
Though I would still recommend shower shoes.
Hot water only lasts so long in the mornings,
After a certain time you might experience cold water issues.

Hallways are unpredictable,
Basically, anything goes.
You might see someone walking their snake,
Or randomly practicing free throws.

Dorm staff is always available,
They're on site day and night.
At 2 in the morning if music is too loud,
Dorm staff might drop in ready to fight.

You can come and go whenever you please,
Ultimately you are only responsible for you.
Everyone has their own lock and key,
Privacy is a commodity to look forward to.

Roommates

Roommates are some of the first people you meet when starting college. Although it is possible to pick a friend to room with when starting college, this is not always an option for everyone. Random roommates are the people who are assigned to a room without knowing each other before hand. Going into college with a friend who becomes a roommate can be difficult if there isn't set boundaries established in advance. Although the transition might be easier when deciding to have a friend as a roommate, friends don't always respect personal space as much as a random person would. For example, it might be easier to tell a random person not to go into your closet than it would be to tell a best friend.

Having a new roommate is a chance to understand what it's like to be exactly where you are, in someone else's shoes. Effective conversation helps roommates get to know each other and understand each other's personalities and perspectives on the world. During the first conversations with a new roommate is the best time to ask about each other's interests and hobbies. These discussions can be used to get a good idea of what to expect the home life to be like over the next several months.

Once solid ground has been established and each roommate knows what to expect from the other, spending time together shouldn't feel like an obligation. It's okay to not immediately want to be around a new roommate. Everyone has their preferences and it shouldn't be taken personally if a roommate prefers to keep to themselves for whatever reason.

"Some people come into our lives and quickly go. Some people stay for a while and leave footprints on our hearts and we are never the same."
-Aaliyah Haughton

Unforgettable

Six different roommates,
All over the course of four years.
Individual people dealing with their own lives,
Managing their own happiness, fighting their own fears.

While I lived my life my way,
I respected how my roommates chose to live theirs.
You never know what to expect,
In a living environment that everyone shares.

I never got used to other people's alarms,
I would always check to make sure it wasn't mine.
It would be six in the morning and I would be up,
Imagine the feeling when I didn't need to be up until nine.

Game nights with roommates are always fun,
Especially when games are won fair and square.
The excitement is endless when everyone's involved,
Imagine the possibilities of the game truth or dare.

There's usually a "mom" of the house,
Somebody that knows how to keep the place clean.
Avoid making unnecessary messes that could make one feel like the maid,
You risk awakening a person you might have never seen.

Roommates are always around,
Sometimes this might drive you insane.
Regardless, when the time comes to officially move out,
You can always appreciate the unforgettable experience you gain.

Romance

Whether or not you have experience with a romantic relationship, college is a place where there are endless opportunities. Romance looks different to everyone. However, the idea of finding a partner with common interests, that likes you as much as you like them is ideal for most.

Many people have goals of meeting their mate within the span of their college years. Although there is no guarantee of whether or not these goals will be achieved, it is important to be aware of the difficulties. Most people in college are going through an "in-between" stage in their life. They are growing and changing and slowly laying the foundation for their future. During this stage, many choices and decisions about life, and with whom it is spent, will be built on a platform that is not yet grounded. An understanding of change and development is important for any successful relationship.

To avoid any confusion, clear communication and an idea of what each person is looking for is an important first step. The infatuation stage that leads people to fall head over heels, just to do a face plant in the dirt, can leave a bad taste for relationships in anyone's mouth. It's also important to practice self-love to make it easier to recognize the kind of love, if any, is being offered by another.

"It's all about falling in love with yourself and sharing that love with someone who appreciates you, rather than looking for love to compensate for a self-love deficit."
–Eartha Kitt

Ear Hustled

Love at first sight,
My experience was love at first sound.
The accent caused an actual buckle sensation,
Before my knees hit the ground.

I heard the words clearly,
Spoken to me harmoniously and slow.
I knew I had found the one,
Simply because my ears said so.

The accent is still memorable,
But only when I imagine it saying words I liked to hear.
Unfortunately, the harmony didn't last,
It didn't take long for the melody to become choppy and insincere.

It really was something,
My ears tricked me into believing I was in love.
The accent was pro-school so my grades were great that semester,
There are worse outcomes I could think of.

Hooking Up

Hooking up has various meanings. It can mean going out for lunch, but it can also be used to describe someone making out in the back of a bar. Either way, it's important to be clear on the subject before things get too serious. Hooking up can be confusing and lead to misunderstandings, wasted time, and hurt feelings.

In any situation, it's important to have an understanding of what hooking up entails. Clear communication keeps you from going into a situation that is intended to be more or less serious than planned. It should be made clear in the beginning what is expected from the interaction and if it has any significant meaning. It's easy to get off to a bad start if you don't start out on the right foot. Knowing the purpose of an interaction in advance allows you to properly prepare or decide if the time being spent is worth it. Being honest with yourself about what you want and don't want is the best way to avoid wasting valuable time.

Everyone has different expectations when it comes to hooking up. It can be disappointing when a situation doesn't meet your assumed expectations. Come to a mutual agreement about what is expected from the experience and be completely honest. Once all the cards are on the table you get the chance to decide whether it's worth it to pass or play.

"Be who you are and say what you feel, because those who mind don't matter, and those who matter don't mind." —Dr. Seuss

Just Chill

I enjoy most of my days alone,
But on this day I decided company would be cool.
I decided to call one of my friends,
Just a nice guy I had met at school.

I drove over to his house,
He met me at the door.
He continued folding his laundry,
While I turned on music and sat with his tablet on the floor.

We didn't have much to talk about,
But of course some words were said.
When the vibes are good, there's no need to fake it,
Forced conversations are dead.

He needed to go to the store,
So on our way we went.
I hopped into the front seat,
Where I would admire the leather and clean car scent.

Upon our return, I laid on the loveseat,
He laid on the couch.
This way we both had our own space,
Enough room for each of us to comfortably slouch.

By the end of the second movie,
I was ready to call it a night.
He walked me to my car,
Then I drove home alone under the moon light.

Budget

Making a budget is necessary to determine how well you work with money. Learning to budget in college can help determine if you need to make any adjustments to ensure your future financial success. Figure out how much money you have to work with, then plan spending around a set amount. Creating a budget makes it easier to keep track of where your money is going and helps avoid spending money you don't have.

"I believe that through knowledge and discipline, financial peace is possible for all of us." -Dave Ramsey

Leftovers

Budgeting is done ideally with cash,
It makes it easier to keep track of spending.
Even when using the mobile bank apps,
They don't always account for the transactions "pending".

Buying fast food should be a luxury,
The price of take-out adds up lightning fast.
The money spent won't even make sense,
Especially when you consider how long it doesn't last.

Determine income and regular expenses for each month,
Write rent or phone bill as "things to pay".
Split the rest between "miscellaneous expenses",
And the funds regularly saved in case of a "rainy day".

The college experience can feel like a huge party. At random times you might find someone bobbing their head to a beat, dancing, or carelessly singing along to a song you may have never heard of. Because every place doesn't have the same channels, it's important to prepare accordingly if you are used to listening to a specific type of music or radio station. Finding an interest in new music during the college experience can lead to an appreciation of the diversity, discussions topics, and medicinal properties that music has to offer.

The music in most parties is intended for everyone to enjoy. This can be a perfect opportunity to find a new song or artist to add to your playlist. Establishing a diverse collection of music can open you up to new cultures and ideas and encourage you to investigate other worlds outside of your own.

Being exposed to various types of music can make it easy to strike up a conversation. The passion for music that most people have will allow them to talk for hours on end. Being well versed on various genres of music can come in handy when discussion topics are scarce.

Music can also have medicinal benefits. This means that by listening to music there is a possibility one can find healing. During times of stress, the right music can be used for calming and meditation. However, all music is not created equal and it is important to choose music wisely when hoping to take advantage of these healing properties.

"Music is a moral law. It gives soul to the universe, wings to the mind, flight to the imagination, and charm and gaiety to life and to everything." - Plato

(Almost) Doctor's Note

Music is the best medicine for the soul,
Research shows it's an ancient sacred cure.
The lyrics teach, and include a tight beat,
The only ingredients I can approve for sure.

The King was a master a melodies,
Produced some of the most powerful tracks I can think of.
Bob Marley, synonymous with a hit,
Compare other pain relievers to singing One Love.

The album Voyage to India by India Arie,
I recommend for problems getting tears to pass.
I also recommend the songs Waves and Devastated,
Various symptoms tend to be relieved with lyrics by Joey BadA$$.

Therapist, currently known as J. Cole,
Conceived cures for problems pertaining to heart.
The results have been quite astounding,
His album 4 Your Eyez Only made a positive impact from the start.

Alex Wiley produced an album known as Tangerine Dream,
Proven to alleviate stress by means of universal knowledge.
Bas counseled me personally with lyrical words of wisdom,
Some of my most meaningful memories of college.

Health

Taking care of personal health care needs may be a new concept that people starting the college experience may not have considered. The risk of physical and mental stress are things that should be taken under consideration while preparing for college.

Taking care of your body during this time can be easy once a plan is established to do so. This includes eating well, working out, and getting adequate rest. Eating well along with drinking plenty of water promotes a healthy immune system. A healthy immune system can protect you against the new germs and bacteria that may be present in the new environment. Working out also helps improve the immune system and can promote mental health when used as a stress reliever. A lack of sleep is another leading cause of a lowered immune system and increases the chances of mental exhaustion.

Cleanliness is important for both mental and physical health. Washing your hands often and disinfecting your surroundings can decrease the chances of getting sick. Having a clean environment can also create a sense of peace and clarity. This can reduce stress and keep you from feeling overwhelmed. If your environment is cluttered during times when you can't think clearly, cleaning up can be a good way to encourage a less foggy sensation.

Mindfulness is the therapeutic practice of accepting one's feelings, thoughts, and bodily sensations. Mindfulness is a state of complete awareness of self and surroundings. Once you are able to use the power of the present to distinguish where the problem is, you are able to actively play a role in finding a solution which can be beneficial for mental and physical health.

"Without health life is not life; it is only a state of languor and suffering - an image of death." -Buddha

Confessions of a College Aged Drama Queen

I'm an emotional eater,
Gaining the freshman fifteen in one semester gave me a clue,
As college went on, my problem got worse,
The first fifteen increased by twenty two.

There's no doubt denial was rough,
I couldn't climb any amount of stairs without breaking a sweat.
I also tried to not to dwell on the embarrassment of the question,
"You due for that baby yet?"

First I decided to cut back on meat,
I know some people think this is crazy.
In return I got clear skin, thick hair, and less fat,
All I got from extra chicken and other meat was tired and lazy.

I also decided to journal daily,
I decided to write down every emotion I could feel.
I was present in each moment and found bliss,
Journaling alone improved my life situation a great deal.

I started doing yoga regularly too,
It has completely transformed my mind and body.
I wish I would've began my practice sooner,
I had deemed it merely a hobby.

I still get emotional when it comes to food,
Nothing about that will change.
However, I wasn't healthy and didn't feel happy,
Not what I had in mind for the college age range.

Organizations and Clubs

Organizations and clubs are a huge hit during college. Between all the sororities and fraternities and Orgsync's extensive list of college involvement opportunities, there will always be ways to get involved. Although getting involved on campus can be a great way to improve your college experience, there should be realistic expectations for what will be gained through campus involvement. Organizations and clubs can be a hassle if the involvement requires significant effort that will take away from time needed to complete school work and other academic responsibilities. It is important to consider the time, energy, and money that may be required when considering joining a club or organization during the college experience.

The time requirement for clubs and organizations should be strongly regarded before making any commitments. Although some time requirements may not appear to be much, the commitment may interfere with time needed to complete class work or studying obligations. Many people who found themselves involved in a number of organizations in high school, may find that the time expectations in college are a lot more extensive than what was previously required. This can make it hard to find time to be involved in several organizations at a time without feeling overwhelmed or stressed.

Taking on the responsibility of a student and participating in organizations on a college campus can be taxing if you aren't able to balance them effectively. Some clubs expect you to be willing and able to give one hundred percent of your effort at all times. Depending on the commitment, not being able to give your full attention to the matter can be harmful, and even dangerous to yourself and others. The amount of energy needed throughout the semester to be successful academically should be strongly considered before making a commitment to any organization.

Some clubs and organizations have fees for membership. These fees can be a onetime thing or they may be required throughout membership. These obligations can be burdensome if you aren't in the position to afford any extra expenses. Finding out about fees ahead of time can save you from experiencing any unnecessary stress in the future.

"Stop letting people who do so little for you control so much of your mind, feelings and emotions." -Will Smith

Options

Getting involved has its perks,
You'll always have something to do.
Show interest and you'll never miss an event,
College clubs always find a way of contacting you.

Club membership can boost a resume,
Leadership positions more than suffice.
Be wary of overbooking your schedule,
Volunteering free time can feel like paying the ultimate price.

Most organizations require members to pay,
Dues and fees are likely to be expected.
No one minds if you participate in all their events,
But without paying dues, a request for a club shirt will certainly be rejected.

Participation is always optional,
Being a member doesn't equate being stuck like glue.
If you decide you don't have the time or have had enough,
Walking away is an option always available to you.

Religion

During the college experience there will be many opportunities to experience different forms of religion and spirituality. Although there is no requirement to be involved in any faith based practice for most colleges, learning about the various belief systems in the world can be intriguing and sometimes life changing. Religion and spirituality is a large part of many people's lives and being able to understand the various belief systems can promote dialogue, discernment, and an opportunity to dissolve division.

Dialogue about religion is important because there are aspects of every belief system that may be misunderstood or misinterpreted. Because it is so easy to become upset and walk away from a conversation about something that is very personal, people tend to avoid these conversations. This is problematic due to the fact that ignorance breeds hate. If people can find a way to put their personal beliefs aside, and learn about and understand someone else's beliefs without allowing it to become a threat to their own, the dialogues can be very educational.

Discernment is the ability to judge well. The ability to judge comes with a clear understanding of a situation from every angle. Without knowledge of the what, where, when, why, and how something came to be, it is inappropriate to make a judgement at all.

The idea that certain topics like religion should be avoided in conversation is directly related to the ignorance that plagues society. If more people were open to discussing the issues that create such conflict, there might be a better chance to dissolve widespread conflict. Open discussions about religion can create an understanding amongst people and decrease the risk of othering. This can dissolve division and allow people to recognize and appreciate each other's differences.

"I prayed for twenty years but received no answer until I prayed with my legs." -Frederick Douglass

Trinity

I always wondered, how is God a jealous God,
If jealousy's a sin?
How do you explain so much empty space in God's house,
When the homeless don't have shelters to sleep in?

I was welcomed into the church family,
I played my appropriate part.
I followed the teachings of the pastor,
While I neglected the temple which housed my heart.

I felt there was something I had forgotten,
Always wondered what that something might be.
A wave of peace preceded pure agony, a tragedy,
For the love of God, I had forgotten me.

Stimulants

Stimulants are substances that raise levels of physiological or nervous activity in the body. Substances in this category include caffeine, alcohol, and a wide variety of prescription and street drugs. Throughout the college experience stimulants are available in various forms. Without proper discretion, developing a dependency on substance use can become a problem. Although the best way to avoid stimulant abuse is to avoid them completely, methods that encourage moderation, oversight, and responsibility, can prevent the development of unhealthy addictions.

Practicing moderation is a way in which an activity is limited or controlled to avoid going to extremes. This can be done by establishing limits for yourself and being aware of tolerance levels. Without clear boundaries set for substance use, it may be difficult to control consumption and can lead to unfavorable outcomes effecting self and others.

If you are unsure of the effect a substance has, or are unaware of tolerance levels for the substance of choice, having someone you trust monitor your use is highly recommended. This person should be trusted enough to call for help if anything unexpected happens and be able to recall events that may be significant. This person should not be thought of as a babysitter and should be respected for their willingness to offer a helping hand.

In order to take responsibility for stimulant use you should know what the substance is, how it effects your body, and why you feel the need to indulge in it. Once you can determine what is happening to you as you partake in the stimulant of choice, it should be determined whether or not you are capable or maintaining use without cause for concern.

"In today's rush, we all think too much, seek too much, want too much, and forget about the joy of just being." -Eckhart Tolle

Commerce

Caffeine is a psychoactive drug,
A central nervous system stimulant based on its chemical makeup.
Tolerance explains how people can drink multiple cups of coffee at a time,
Yet still can't seem to be able to wake up.

It is quite difficult to vilify drugs,
The most harmful seem to be legally regulated.
Research on popular stimulants can be rather disturbing,
Often reducing the urge to be artificially stimulated.

Multiple Workloads

Pursuing employment during the college experience can be a potential challenge. However, prioritizing responsibilities will promote organization, which can increase productivity despite multiple commitments. Taking on the responsibility of a student as well as an employee should involve preparation, production, and patience.

Preparing for assignments and exams ahead of time is beneficial when working a job is necessary. Being aware of academic responsibilities in advance allows you to use free time appropriately and spread out the workload. This awareness decreases the chances of becoming overwhelmed and falling behind in academic responsibilities. Verifying deadlines and checking for schedule updates regularly can increase the chances of academic success.

Using time wisely to ensure the production of favorable grades on assignments requires taking initiative and having the motivation to succeed. Taking initiative ensures there is an understanding of what needs to be done and the amount of effort required to achieve success. Diligence is equally needed to maintain motivation to see the efforts through to completion. Being able to fulfill the duties of a student and an employee demands a drive for success.

Patience is needed as a student employee to maintain sanity. It can be overwhelming at times to have multiple workloads all at once. However, being able to practice patience with yourself in knowing the situation is temporary can make things a lot easier.

"I only want to do what I really want to do; otherwise, I'm content to sit here and play my guitar all day." - Eddie Murphy

Fulltime Student

I needed a job through college,
I was responsible for paying my own bills.
I admit I also worked to have extra money on the side,
I like to treat myself and Chipotle was a regular luxury meals.

The hours weren't much,
And I was nowhere near full time,
But when I was questioned about my grades at the end of semester,
You'd think I picked up a job as a circus mime.

I didn't practice good study habits,
School had never been too hard for me.
After one semester of college with a part time job,
Being a college student had to become my top priority.

Any opportunity where people are involved is an opportunity to make a new friend. Social events that actively promote face to face interactions are good places to start when seeking new friends during the college experience.

Game nights like Bingo is an example of some of the activities colleges may organize to assist students in making new friends. These are controlled environments where no one is expecting anything from you and you can take as much time as you need to warm up to the new crowd. Volunteering to do anything to help during the night will instantly get you attention and make people want to get to know who you are. This works well for people who are outgoing and like to be the center of attention. However, if you're the type to sit too quiet, for too long, you'll inevitably be the center of attention at some point for just being "too quiet". For the best results in these situations, show up early and sit right in the middle of the room. That way, people will have to sit next to you, making it easier to blend in and you'll always get the best view of who you're most likely compatible with.

It's important to remember that friends are the people that should support and encourage you on your journey. They shouldn't be judgmental or make you feel bad for being you. Friendships should provide a mutual love and respect for one another at all times. If you ever have to question the love and respect being given or received from yourself or another person, it is best to take a step back and reevaluate the friendship.

"Friendship is the hardest thing in the world to explain. It's not something you learn in school. But if you haven't learned the meaning of friendship, you really haven't learned anything." — Muhammad Ali

Buds

Thinking of the friends I've had,
They've all taught me lessons about life.
For example happy people spread love and laughter,
While people with hardened hearts tend to be quicker to reach for a knife.

Although I don't remember the names of all the friends I've had,
I can still picture the numerous faces.
I will forever cherish memories of incredible conversations,
While marveling in memories of friends accompanying me to some of the
most unforgettable places.

You can't judge a book by its cover,
Because a friend by the looks, you'll never know.
True friends are able to appreciate one another's differences,
And are capable of watching one another grow.

For a friendship to flourish,
It must be planted with a solid foundation.
Grounded with love and respect,
Watered with honest communication.

Some friendships have gone sour,
For a few I will admit to blame.
For others I'll call a Spade a Spade,
Simply because I refuse to be manipulated by any mind game.

Some friends will grow a part,
While others will decide to leave.
But when friendships die, the memories don't,
So to heal, time is needed to grieve.

Humanities

The human race as a whole is described as humanity. It is important to recognize the immensely diverse frames of reference that make up the humanities and how it is directly related to what college has to offer. The diversity can be attributed to social class, intellect, ethnicity, nationality, interest, and preference. The college experience is a representation of what the humanities are and promote an appreciation for perspective, procedure, and purpose.

Acknowledging different perspectives within the human race has the ability to encourage curiosity that can lead to uncovering history and truths about a wide variety of topics. Being aware of past events can establish a foundation for understanding people and patterns that may have otherwise been overlooked. New knowledge has the ability to promote positive progress and encourage improvements in various situations.

The humanities illustrate the idea that there is no one right way to achieve success. The procedure leading to success among the human race has proved to be based on putting in the necessary work to acquire a favorable outcome. The procedure for success can vary and proves the inevitable chance for success when the chance for failure is removed as a possibility.

The human race displays a wide range of talents and capabilities. This compilation of diverse viewpoints has created and maintained the current society. A recognition of each person's specific contribution can enable an understanding of humanity's reason for existence. The college experience creates wonderful opportunities to develop a personal take on humanity's purpose.

"People don't want to hear the truth, they never do. They wanna live in some kind of fantasy. And then when they get caught up in it, they start being in denial because they don't want to be wrong." - Paul Mooney

Black Sheep

All animals are a part of the same family,
All various shapes, colors, and sizes.
I wonder if the other creatures ever forgave Mother Nature,
For her little human surprises.

It had to be rough after humanity came along,
With their egos and complicated minds.
Disrupting the natural peace of just being,
Ruining the joy of living and wreaking havoc of all kinds.

It's fascinating how humans think they're different,
Essentially every species is the same.
All here for the same purpose,
To enhance the overall quality of the game.

Taking on the college experience promotes change and requires the courage to step out of one's comfort zone. It is a big step from one stage of life into another. During this time away from home there will be an opportunity to establish independence, discover new opportunities, and gain an enhanced perspective on life as a whole.

College fosters an environment that promotes self-sufficiency. It helps bridge the gap between adolescence and adulthood. Students are forced to find their own way. They must learn to survive on their own and choose the life they want to live. Independence is established by going into the world alone and believing in one's ability to succeed.

The discoveries that can be made during a college experience are never ending. Every day has the potential to open the door to a new opportunity or fulfill a lifelong dream. There is no cap on the experiences that can be had during college and the sooner one realizes that the better. With the combination of new people, places, and a thirst for excitement, the possibilities are endless.

During the time spent in college there is a lot of potential for change. Although change can be uncomfortable at times, it is necessary for growth. Growth in any capacity alters the way in which situations and circumstances are perceived. Perspectives can change drastically between the time of college admission and the time of college graduation. It is important to recognize how important growth is to ensure a clear perspective of life and it's infinite opportunities.

"Comparing yourself to someone else really stops you from being who you are." –Alicia Keys

Gas

There's no place like home,
Of course I knew what that meant.
I'd always have a place to go back to,
Even if I move away and start paying my own rent.

My city is still there,
In my absence it remained the same.
It's amazing that I'm the one who's different now,
Only recognizable by the name.

I grew up in college,
Maturity turned out to be a pleasant surprise.
I gained significant life experience,
Long story short, college made me wise.

Home is where the heart is,
Never to be left behind when you go.
It's the strength that will keep you going,
As well as the fuel for the fire that forces you to grow.

"The only real change comes from inside." – Jermaine Cole

ABOUT THE AUTHOR

Kayla Burrell developed her writing ability over many years. Although she had always had a passion for writing, it wasn't until her senior year in college that she decided she wanted to be a writer. Through her college experience, Kayla Burrell was able to interpret her true heart's desire and established herself as an author.

87737318R00048

Made in the USA
Lexington, KY
30 April 2018